BRAINSTORM!

Wendy Ashton Shimkofsky

Designed & illustrated by Loris Lesynski

Pembroke Publishers Limited

To ELiot, Carrie and Aaron – dreams come true.

Wendy Ashton Shimkofsky

To aLL the kids with imagination – keep it up!

Loris Lesynski

© 1997 Wendy Ashton Shimkofsky, text
© 1997 Loris Lesynski, illustration

Pembroke Publishers
538 Hood Road
Markham, Ontario, Canada
L3R 3K9

Canadian Cataloguing in Publication Data

Shimkofsky, Wendy Ashton
      Brainstorm! : amazing ideas and astounding puzzles to stretch your brain

ISBN 1-55138-031-5

1. Puzzles – Juvenile literature.   I. Lesynski, Loris.
II. Title.

GV1493.S55 1996   j793.73   C96-931061-7

Design: Loris Lesynski/MPD & Associates

Printed and bound in Canada
9 8 7 6 5 4 3 2 1

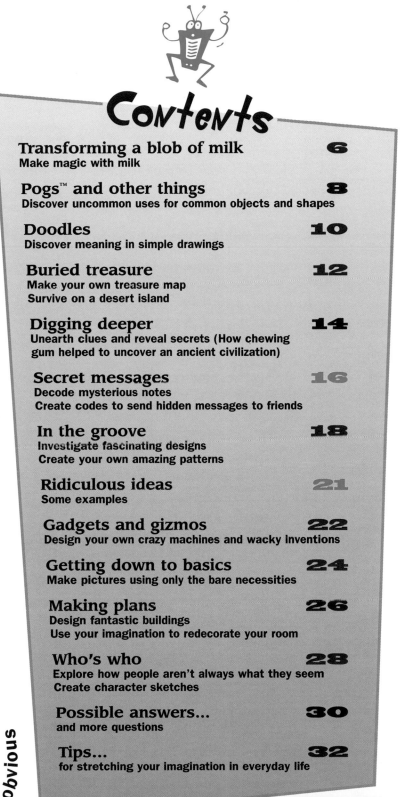

Contents

Avoid the obvious

shoes had wings?

What if people could crawl up walls and over ceilings as spiders do?

What if you could travel to the edge of the universe?

The world needs **curious** kids!

INTRODUCTION

Asking **"what if?"** to stretch your imagination is what this book is about. You can create **mysterious codes** to send hidden messages, design **fantastic buildings**, or redesign your room. You can transform milk, or create character sketches for your **stories.**

Go ahead, ask "what if?" and find out what ideas this book offers you. There are no rules allowed here — anything goes — but these tips can help to get you started. Let yourself daydream to give **your imagination** a chance to explore different ways of looking at things.

Have fun making a list of **ridiculous ideas** that might lead to something useful.

Relax and let your ideas flow. You can find more tips at the end of the book, but don't forget, your imagination is better than any tips **anyone** can give you.

What if each classroom had **25 teachers** and **1 student?**

Sometimes your imagination feels like this...

and other times like this!

Brainstorming loosens up
your imagination and fills your head with amazing ideas.
You can use these ideas to **change the world**.
Brainstorm away!

TRANSFORMING A BLOB OF MILK

You aren't supposed to cry over spilled milk, but is there anything interesting you can do with it? You could use it to attract cats, or you can use its shape to give you an idea for a drawing. Let's see what the illustrator can do with a the blob of spilled milk on this page. All it will take is some simple lines, a bit of color, and a lot of imagination. Can you guess what it will be? Does the shape give you any ideas? Jot down your guesses.

Inspiration comes from the most unexpected places.

What if you tried to transform milk into something totally different? Pour two cups of milk (or cream) into a plastic jar or a container with a tightly fitting lid. Stir in half a cup of sugar. Seal the container tightly and then put it into a large bag that has a "zipper" to close it, or use a larger plastic container with a tight lid. Fill the rest of the large bag with clean snow or crushed ice. Sprinkle four tablespoons of salt onto the ice. Seal the bag and shake it.

Keep shaking until something wonderful happens (about ten minutes) or pop it into the freezer for twenty minutes, shaking it occasionally. The milk doesn't even look the same anymore just because, instead of drinking it, you poured it into a jar, added a couple of things, and gave it a shake. Now instead of a blob of milk, you have dessert!

IMAGINE how you could transform **other things** — a block of wood, an icicle, a cookie sheet, or a box.

What if you cut pieces out, or added legs or feathers?

What if you **sat** on your object, or held it over your head?

Find **TEN** other ordinary objects around your house or school room that could be used in interesting ways.

If you could build your house out of ice cream, what topping would you choose for your room?

POGS™ AND OTHER THINGS

Who invented POGS™?

Children did. In the days when milk came in glass bottles, kids discovered that the bottle-cap liners were great for playing games. Then, in 1991, a Hawaiian school teacher, who had played with the cardboard cap liners when she was a kid, taught her students one of these old games. She used caps from a local company's fruit drink. The caps were stamped with the initials of the **P**assionfruit, **O**range and **G**uava drink. Now thousands of children play POGS™ and collect and trade cap liners all around the world. All this fun because kids asked "what if?" about disks that most people would have just considered **garbage!**

If you Look around, you might find things you can use for games: rubber bands, plastic bottles, cereal boxes, bottle caps, an old comb, or sticks left from a backyard clean-up. You can find all kinds of uses for some of these ordinary things.

What do you think kids will be collecting from garbage in 2050?

For examPle, how many ways can you use a stick? Sticks come in a variety of shapes and sizes. What can you do with sticks that have odd shapes? What if you attach other things to the sticks?

Toothpicks are tiny sticks. What if you use some glue with toothpicks? What can you make?

Now let's tackle something more abstract — circles. You can begin by thinking about different kinds of circles. You can draw a circle with a pencil, or make it from a flexible twig from a bush, or from wet clay. What else could you use to make circles? A circle can be solid like a doorknob, or hollow like a hoop. It can be as tiny as a button or as large as a spaceship. Look around your school room or your house to find different ways circles are used.

Imagine

What could you make from 5,000 pencil stubs, or from an old leather glove?

What could you make with twist ties, or from plastic bread-bag tabs, or discarded computer disks?

What would you call a robot designed to eat useless garbage?

DooooooooodLES

Have you ever found

yourself making funny little marks or doodling with your pencil?

Doodling might seem like a great way to waste time, but it can be useful, too.

Take a close look at the cake in this illustration. The elaborate designs on it are all just simple doodles joined together. The side border is nothing more complicated than a series of half circles and little ovals.

Can you see a row of **Cs** or a diamond with an **S** on either side? Try to spot the other doodles that the baker used to add the finishing touches to the cake.

Every list of outrageous ideas has the start of **at least one** great idea.

The doodles on the cake are simply used as decoration, but there are also other kinds of doodles, like the ones on this page. The meaning these doodles have for you could be entirely different from the meaning other people see.

For example, you might think the round doodle with the smaller circle inside is a bunny's tail, but other people might see a big yawn, the start button on a time machine, a belly button, or a snowman seen from above. If you look at them upside down, do you get any different ideas? If you looked out the window of an airplane and saw two large grass-covered circles in the middle of a field, what would you suppose they were? Could they be the remains of an ancient castle, or the spot where a spaceship landed long ago? How many possibilities can you think of?

Try creating some new doodles of your own. You can get some great ideas by looking at things from unusual angles. For example, to get started, lie on the floor and look at the shape of a floor lamp from below, or a rocking chair, or a stool. Draw doodles of these.

You can also draw doodles of people. How would you sketch a doodle of someone peering over a fence, or someone sweeping the sidewalk with a broom? What doodles could you create of your cat?

When you have a page of doodles, show it to your friends and have them **guess** what each one is.

If last names had to rhyme with **first names**, what would your new name be?

BURIED TREASURE

In 1795, three teenagers began a treasure hunt that has lasted for over 200 years. People say that Oak Island, Nova Scotia, is where the pirate Captain Kidd buried chests filled with coins, jewelry, and precious gems.

Each time searchers dug down below a certain level, the hole filled with water and no amount of pumping could get rid of it. The workers were forced to stop. It seemed that the pirates had arranged a booby trap to protect their booty. The booby trap worked so well that, although the search has cost over $10 million dollars, no treasure has been found...*yet.*

Legend says that when all the oaks are gone from Oak Island and seven people have died, the treasure will be found.

Today, there are no oaks left on Oak Island and six people have lost their lives searching for the treasure.

Could you

guard treasure as well as the Oak Island pirates? Let's find out! Imagine your own pirate adventures.

Your pirate ship is sinking! You save one chest and row to shore in a small boat. The island appears deserted.

What will you do first? Write down some ideas, but remember that the island has no telephones, no restaurants, and no banks.

Are you curious about the treasure chest? Is it filled with riches, food, old clothes, or school books? It can hold anything you want (or something you *don't* want).

Your imagination can take you farther than your feet.

Taking care of yourself on a deserted island is harder than it is at home. What could you find to eat? What materials on the island could you use to make a safe, dry house? What **else** should you do? How could you get help?

How will you keep your treasure safe? If you decide to hide the chest or bury it, you should make a treasure map. You'll need some landmarks to help guide you. List things that might be on your island and think of secret names for any you could use. A waterfall might be "tear drops" or a field of grass might be "green whiskers." Note these landmarks on your map, decide where your treasure will be hidden, and then make a list of clues such as "ten paces north of Finger Rock."

After finishing your map, see if your friends or family can locate your treasure using only the map and clues.

Next, dream up a few booby traps to protect it.

If you had to choose three things from your room to be buried in a time capsule, what would they be?

DIGGING DEEPER

Chewing Gum Leads to Amazing Discoveries

An expedition in 1848 to find sap from sapodilla trees in the dense rain forests of Guatemala led to a surprise. Instead of finding the sap, which is the main ingredient in chewing gum, the men came upon the ruin of ancient buildings. For thirteen years, people carefully examined the entire area. All together, they discovered 3,000 buildings and a wealth of information about the Mayans, the people who had once lived there.

Those who study the objects left by earlier peoples are called **archeologists.** Everything they find, whether it's an arrowhead or ashes from a fire, is a clue that helps them understand the past a little better. Archeologists sift through tons of soil to uncover bits of history.

People like making rules to get things done, but have they tried **ideas** and **daydreams** and **fun?**

Artifact: Details:

Broken porcelain teacup found in the vegetable garden. Gold rim. Maybe from a garden tea party long ago?

Teddy bear found in the den cupboard. Maybe it was once a baby's room?

...ften pantry

You can get an idea

of what an archeologist's work is like when you dig up the garden in spring. Use a piece of old screen or just your hands to sift through the soil. Bits of broken glass or china tell you what kind of dishes previous owners of the place used. Old square nails could give you a clue to the age of an old shed or house that had been there. You might find pieces of bone, rusty screws, or sea shells. What would these clues tell you?

The soil is not the only place to look for clues to the past. Your house or apartment can tell you a lot about previous owners. If you found a pacifier, a cotton swab, and a baby rattle in the corner of a closet, what would these tell you?

How about a toothless comb or a bottle of cough syrup?

What could you learn from an old shopping list, a grocery store receipt, a piece of macaroni, and a dry-cleaning bill?

ExpLore

You might enjoy exploring your own past, too. **What clues** can you find in an old trunk or from family photo albums?

How about looking in "catch-all" drawers, under the sofa cushions, or under your bed, behind your dresser, or in the corners of closets?

What might your exploration uncover about **your** history?

Uses for a knight's helmet: bird's nest? baby's bathtub? dog dish? toy box? hamster's cage? flower pot? lunch box?

SECRET MESSAGES

Imagine that one day as you walk through
the woods, you discover a large circular clearing. The grass is a very bright, almost neon, green. In the middle of the circle is a glowing object. You can see that something is written on the object. It looks like this:

Who put the object in the clearing, and why? Who could have written these strange letters? What could they mean? Examine each of the symbols carefully.

In some languages, symbols represent whole words or thoughts. Do these remind you of anything? Look at the first symbol. Could it be waves or perhaps mountains? The "tail" at the right side of the second symbol seems to be pointing forward. What could this part mean?

After you have studied the symbols, make up a message or story based on the symbols.

There's a clue to the code hidden on this page.

Look at the title again. Each symbol represents a letter of the alphabet. Note where a symbol is used in relation to other symbols. Are some often side by side? Are the squares identical? Are the diamonds all the same size and width?

Some symbols look alike, but they're different. Are there any double letters? Do some often appear at the beginning or end of the word? In our language, the letter **e** is one of the most commonly used letters. Is any symbol used more than the others? Substitute the letter **e** for it and see if you can figure out the message.

The key to this code is on page 30.

Daydreaming is a great pastime because you can do it anywhere.

People who write and solve messages in secret code are called **cryptographers.** They use ideas similar to the ones you just used. Cryptographers have to know which letters are found together often, and which combinations could end or start a word. Have you ever noticed a word that started with 'BK' or ended in 'RW'? You're more likely to find a word that begins with 'BR' or one that ends with 'RK.' Certain letters go together better than others. A cryptographer uses this knowledge to find **meaning** in a group of apparently meaningless **symbols.**

You can also create a code by using everyday words in a different way. *Here's a sample:*

speak ↑

means speak up.

Can you solve these messages?

↑ ___	ban/ ana	CALM ↓	STAND ___
___ BOARD	_BUT_ ___	TROUBLE TROUBLE	SCHEDULE │
IMAGE IWVCE	sisters sisters	right / time	time time

Create

Using codes is a great way to disguise messages. Instead of using the alphabet to spell out words, replace everyday words or letters with pictures or symbols.

You could make a code of your own and write a **secret** message to a friend.

Oak Island's Secret Message

In 1803 when treasure hunters tunnelled down ninety feet, they discovered a large flat stone with strange symbols carved into it. Some people believe the secret message is: **Forty feet below two million pounds are buried.** What do you think?

IN THE GROOVE

I LOVE THIS TUNE!

If someone handed you a long-playing record or a compact disc with the label covered up, how could you tell what music was on it? An American doctor, Arthur Lintgen, taught himself to identify the music simply by looking at the grooves on classical albums. Dr. Lintgen realized that the grooves formed patterns that could tell him about the music, including which instruments were being played and how loud the music was. If Dr. Lintgen had merely listened to the records, we might never have heard of him. Instead, he tried a different approach and amazed people with his ability to "read" the patterns.

You might not always notice, but patterns surround you. Numbers can form patterns and so can letters. Some are difficult to spot (like the ones on records or CDs), and others are much easier (like flowers on wallpaper). Some patterns can be arranged to become "brain teasers." Look at these patterns. These two groups have certain things in common.

They are both made up of letters. Each letter is followed by a space and then another letter. That's a pattern. The two groups are also different from each other. Group A is made up of capital letters; Group B has all small, or lower-case, letters. If you print a sample from each group, you might notice another difference in the way the letters are formed.

GROUP A
F H I K L M N T V X Y Z

GROUP B
a b c d e g j o p q r s u

Every second of the day, someone, somewhere, gets a new idea. Have you had yours today?

What patterns can you see in the next two groups?

GROUP #1	GROUP #2
1 4 7	2 3 5 8

If you were looking at the shapes of the numbers, where would you put the number 9?

Now look at these examples. How are the two groups different? Where would the letter Z fit?

GROUP X

L T V X

GROUP Y

A F H K N Y

Hint: Try printing one letter from each group.

These numbers have something in common with the words.

1881   6009   1691   1961   SOS   tOOt

Hint: If you turn the book upside down (or stand on your head) you might discover it.

There is something special about these examples.

**101   131   313   1661   1991   2002
MOM   TOT   WOW**

Hint: Turning this puzzle upside down won't help, but you do need to look at it in a different way. Any questions? Try looking at the words in the mirror.

What would happen if suddenly the English alphabet had one more letter?

Imagine

If people walked on their **hands**, how would pockets have to be redesigned?

MORE GROOVING

Making patterns of your own can be a lot of fun, and sometimes it's easier than trying to solve someone else's. Here are a few suggestions to get you started.

★ Find some words, phrases, sentences, or numbers that read the same backwards and forwards. They're called **palindromes.**

> Hey! You can read this either way. WOW!

TOO HOT TO HOOT

Numbers and short words are the easiest to start with **(Bob, did, bib)**. If you want to try a phrase, you need words that are also words when you read them backwards, such as **gum** and **mug**, **evil** and **live**, **on** and **no**. Find as many as you can and then try to put some together into a phrase. (You'll probably have to leave out words like **a** and **the** or it won't work.) Here are a few:

Dennis sinned.

Niagara or roar again.

A Toyota

★ Sometimes patterns are more obvious when you only look at a small portion. What are **these** patterns part of? (Answers are on page 30.)

★ Numbers and letters aren't the only things you can use to make patterns. Try some materials you have around the house. Sprinkle rice or sand on a piece of dark paper. Create a design with your finger or let a design form naturally by moving the paper. When you study the patterns, what do you see? This is a great time to let your mind wander freely. Explore every small section and then examine the whole picture. The images might change if you look at it from another viewpoint. For example, if you turn the page to one side, then to the other, do you see different pictures? Trade your ideas with your friends and see how they interpret the patterns you created.

RIDICULOUS IDEAS
SOME EXAMPLES

Dale C's
ABSURD IDEAS

- automatic shoelaces that tie and untie themselves
- desks on top of each other like bunkbeds, so schools have more floor space
- you have to play video games to get good grades at school

THINGS I THINK THE WORLD NEEDS:

- a self-cleaning room
- a hat anchor for windy days
- vegetables that taste like hamburgers
- water slides to take you to school
- electric head warmers identical to your hair
- chocolate toothpaste

Lesley's
SILLY SUGGESTIONS

Invent a cement that combines with old coffee grounds and teabags to make cheap, long-lasting bike paths in parks.

Invent a video game that works only when you have a cold.

Lee W's
AMAZING NOTIONS

- Drinking glasses are made of ice.
- People have to pick a favorite color and wear only that color for a whole month.
- Parents have to get Mom and Dad licences renewed once a year just like driver's licences.

Chris's
LIST OF RIDICULOUS POSSIBILITIES

- invisible playing cards so no one can see your hand
- all plates and cups made of dessert wafers so you can eat them after you've finished your supper
- a remote control on your hockey puck
- a beeper to warn you of approaching bullies

Who invented socks? Who invented shoes? Who invented bubblegum? Who invented glues?

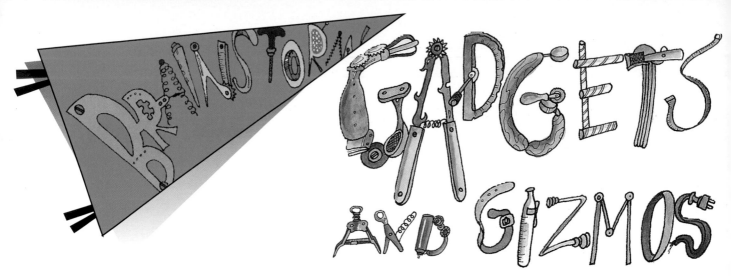

GADGETS AND GIZMOS

Inventions seem to make the impossible possible. Can you imagine being the person to see the first television? How amazing it must have been to see things happening in a box! Or how about saving television programs to watch at a more convenient time? That would have seemed like magic.

Television wouldn't be as much fun without the inventions that came afterward such as the video recorder and video games, and, of course, the remote control.

Inventions are new gadgets that allow people to do things that were once difficult or impossible. How does a person come up with fresh ideas for inventions? Curiosity plays a large part — people often see a problem and wonder how they can solve it.

For example, in 1922, at the age of fifteen, J. Armand Bombardier tried to find a way to make travelling across snow easier. He put a car engine on an old sleigh, added a propeller, and created the first snow machine. After years of improving on his idea, he patented the snowmobile, and eventually he formed his own company to manufacture the machines.

Start writing "I really wish someone would invent a - - - -"
just to find out what you'll say next!

There must be all kinds of other things that people could use that have not yet been invented. What tasks do you have that you want a new tool or machine for?

What about a machine to automatically feed your cat or dog? Or a device to transport your dirty laundry into the washing machine? Think of other gadgets you could use and sketch a design for them.

The contraptions in the following illustration certainly are wild and wacky. What do you suppose they were designed to do?

Imagine

useless inventions...

- a tuxedo for a penguin
- stilts for fish
- new socks full of holes
- silent drums
- wheels for kites

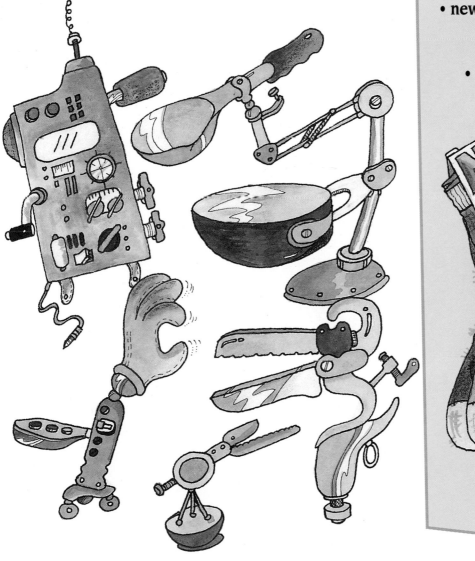

Getting Down to Basics

Some people are squares, others are hearts, ovals, or rectangles. Which are you? To find out, stand in front of a mirror. Outline your face on the mirror with lipstick or something easy to wipe off. What shape have you drawn? Your eyes are oval, your mouth is round, and your nose is triangular.

Just like your face, everything around you is made up of basic shapes. Sometimes they are easy to spot, like the squares and rectangles that make up a sofa. At other times, details make the basic shape harder to pick out. A dog is basically a rectangle with four thinner rectangles for legs and a circle-head covered in fur.

Many illustrators plan their sketches with simple shapes. You could do this too. **Start** with the basic form and then use lines to fill in the details and soften the original picture.

You can **erase** your first outline to clean up your sketch.

See if you can spot the basic shapes that make up other objects. Copy the shapes on this page onto another piece of paper, cut them out, and move them around to make different designs and pictures. To make a person out of shapes, you need a circle for the head, a rectangle for the body, long rectangles for the arms and legs, and small squares for the hands and feet.

What other pictures can you make using these shapes? You could try more complicated scenes.

What shapes would you need to show someone sitting at a computer, or a child fishing, or a person chopping wood?

Can you spot the basic shapes that make up the objects in the room where you are sitting?

MAKING PLANS

Sarah Winchester was worried about evil spirits. A psychic told her that as long as she continued building her house, the evil spirits would not bother her. Today, Winchester House in California is in the record books as the home under construction for the longest time. Work began in 1886 and went on 24 hours a day for 38 years. The eight-room farmhouse turned into a mansion with 40 bedrooms, 13 bathrooms, six kitchens, 10,000 windows, and 2,000 doorways and closets. Some of the 40 staircases lead nowhere, others take you back where you started. Doors open onto thin air or blank walls. The building has trap doors and secret passage-ways. It was all meant to confuse the ghosts who must have been too busy getting lost to scare Mrs. Winchester.

...and next...

Buildings usually start with an architect's drawings and plans, whether they're farmhouses or mansions built for ghosts. All you need is a blank piece of paper and a pencil, and you can design something as fantastic as Winchester House. How about a space-age recreation centre, a carnival fun house, or a medieval castle? Let your imagination go wild. After you've finished, try your hand at decorating the building.

Do you believe in ghosts? Do ghosts believe **in you?**

What if you were to redesign your bedroom? Do you dream of sleeping in an Egyptian pyramid or a jungle tree house? Pick up your pencil and turn your room into anything you want. Choose a piece of paper that has the same proportions as your room — a square sheet for a square room and a rectangular sheet for a rectangular room. It might help to use paper with squares already marked on it (graph paper).

Measure your room and your furniture. Choose a unit of measurement and scale it down to a small unit of measurement that will fit on your paper.

Draw your furniture to scale on a piece of paper and cut it out. Move the pictures of your furniture around on your room plan until you are pleased with the result. Next, trace the arrangement onto a clean sheet of paper and sketch in the details you want.

a new look in your room with just a few simple and inexpensive changes. Use pieces of fabric and objects you already have instead of buying new things. A ten-gallon hat, a lasso, and a suede vest — and your room's a western bunkhouse. Or set up camp with glow-in-the-dark stars (or stars painted on the ceiling), a fishing rod, and a blanket "tent" over your bed. When you finish your plans on paper, show them to your **parents.** By using your imagination, you can give your room **a new look** without spending money.

Even if you like the way your room looks now, you can still have fun playing with new room designs on paper.

WHO'S WHO?

Have you ever looked at people rushing around and wondered why they were in such a hurry or where they were going?

Imagine unusual names and uncommon occupations for them, or imagine them to be characters in a mystery.

Do people's names influence their occupations? There's Candace Sweet, the candymaker, and B. A. Doctor, the pediatrician and . . .

CouLd the man wearing a track suit be a spy or the woman carrying a briefcase, an international jewel thief?

Could the person in the clown suit at a birthday party be an astronaut or a professional weed grower? No, you can't always know people by their appearance, but by observing them you can learn a lot. Writers sometimes listen in on conversations in restaurants and watch how people act to get ideas for developing story characters.

Look at the people in the illustration and try to imagine what their lives are like. Describe how they talk and laugh, and how they walk. Are their houses messy or tidy? What are their favorite foods? How do they treat their friends? What jobs do they have? What makes each one different from everybody else? Writers often ask themselves questions like these about the characters in their books to make them come alive. The writers' answers form clear pictures, or character sketches, of people in fiction.

Create your own **character sketches** of the people in the illustration using the questions as a guide.

What are their lives like? How do they talk and laugh? How do they walk? Are they messy or tidy? What are their favorite foods? How do they treat their friends? What are their jobs? What makes each different?

What would happen if every day had one more hour?

POSSIBLE ANSWERS... perhaps you dreamed up others?

POGS™ ... (page 8)

Just a few of the many things you could do or make with A STICK: tent pole, rolling pin, ski, magic wand, game piece, build furniture, "limbo" under, find water, spell words, roast hot dogs, dry laundry, pitch hay…

CIRCLES: ball, lid, hat, plate, lamp base, wheel, planet, bingo marker, doll's eyes, picture frame, cage, cookie, eyeglasses, ice rink, train animal to jump through…

COOKIE SHEET: slide on it, make a table, a tray, a shield, a rain catcher, a hat…

WOOD: ramp, seat, drum, stage, stand on it…

ICICLE: stir a drink, melt it for water, make a nose for a snowman…

BOX: store treasures, hide in it, pretend it's a ship or a car, make a puppet theatre, planter…

DOODLES (page 10)

What some people see in the doodles:

… looking down a large hat

… a cat passing a doorway

… a bear climbing a tree

… someone scrubbing the floor

… the sides of two balls viewed in a microscope

… a snake on the road

… an elephant walking away

… an army crossing a covered bridge

… a man in a hammock with a book in his pocket

… a giraffe passing a window

… a bubble-gum champ

… earmuffs for a rabbit

… a centipede with its legs crossed

SECRET MESSAGES (page 16)

a	b	c	d	e	f	g	h	i	j	k	l	m
✴	★	◉	♥	α	⚡	✗	℘	●	✚	℔	❖	◆

n	o	p	q	r	s	t	u	v	w	x	y	z
✳	℗	✳	!	❏	➜	❐	⌗	◆	☊	♣	=	✪

SECRET CODE (page 17)

line up	banana split	calm down	understand
over board (or above board)	but(t)on	double trouble	behind schedule
mirror image	twin sisters	right on time	time after time

IN THE GROOVE (page 18)

The letters in Group A are all made with straight lines.

In Group B, they can all be printed without lifting up the pencil; they are all made with curves.

In Group 1, the numbers are all made with straight lines. You add 3 to each number to get the next one: $1 + 3 = 4$, $4 + 3 = 7$.

The numbers in Group 2 all have curves. The number pattern is a little harder: $2(+1)$ $3(+2)$ $5(+3)$ 8.

Group X: The letters have two straight lines.

Group Y: The letters have three straight lines.

Z belongs in Group Y.

The numbers like 1881 and the words like SOS read the same upside down. Numbers like 101 and words like MOM read the same backwards.

MORE GROOVING (page 20)

The patterns are part of:

1 a country road

2 a stone wall

3 a hammock, upside down

4 a sweater

5 a spider web

6 clown hair

7 outside wall of an old cottage

8 upside down picnic basket

More palindromes:

Was it Eliot's toilet I saw?

Enid and Edna dine.

There's more than one answer to almost every question.

& MORE QUESTIONS

Do you think more interesting thoughts when you are upside down?

HEEHEE... 12 ÷ 4... HA HA HA... = 3!! HO HO HO

What kind of new equipment would your classroom need if people learned best when they giggled?

Can you identify books with your eyes closed, just by feeling the covers?

Which would you choose — superhearing or x-ray vision?

Where do stars go for vacation?

If you could train your dog or cat to take over one of your chores at home, **which one** would it be?

What if... **dogs** ruled the world?

Suppose you had to make a choice once a year between a week of snow in July or a week of scorching heat in January. Which would you choose?

You have had a **blizzard** and the snow is as high as you are tall. You have no snow shovel. **What** can you use to dig yourself out?

TIPS FOR STRETCHING YOUR IMAGINATION IN EVERYDAY LIFE

BRAINSTORM!

Relax and let your mind wander.

Write down all the ideas, words, or images that come to you.

Treat **all** your ideas as being of **equal** value.

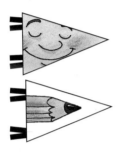

Ask **"what if?"** questions to help yourself look at things in different ways.

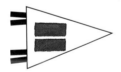

Give your ideas a chance to **grow**.

Try a **different approach** if you have trouble with an idea — imagine changing colors, shapes, sounds, and textures to create something new.